The Clouds Go Down To Heaven

Also by Robin Sinclair and published by Ginninderra Press
Haiku Diary (Pocket Poets)

Robin Sinclair

The Clouds Go Down To Heaven

Acknowledgements

The following haiku appeared in an Artist's Book by Janet Ayliffe: The river pool…, Crumbs of earth still cling…, Black cockatoos…, On a leafless branch…, In the pre-dawn dark…, Slender willow twigs…, Among the violets…

The following appeared in *HOBO* poetry and haiku magazine in 1997–8: A wrinkle of smoke…, Silvereye hovers…, A strand of web…

These appeared in *Yellow Moon*, 1997: Summer's litter…, After rain…, Leaves flutter and fall…, Somewhere a bronzewing…

Salisbury Writers' Festival Awards for haiga (illustrated haiku): Winter's tears…, An inch of ripple…

In *Walking Cheerfully*, the South Australian Quaker newsletter: Fragrance of peaches…, 'Do not disturb'…, The river pool…, On every twig-tip…, Woodsmoke and music…

To go with paintings by Glen Ash: Fruit and Veg Haiku

In *The Independent Weekly*, 16 April 2010: The Sleeping Giant, The Garden of the Sleeping Giant

The Clouds Go Down To Heaven
ISBN 978 1 74027 676 4
Copyright © Robin Sinclair 2011

First published 2011
Reprinted 2015

GINNINDERRA PRESS
PO Box 3461 Port Adelaide SA 5015
www.ginninderrapress.com.au

Contents

What is a haiku?	6
At Home in the Adelaide Hills	7
The Seasons	9
Observed in Passing	23
Unseasonal Haiku	25
The Discussion Group: haiku in response to issues	26
Fruit and Veg Haiku	28
On the Road in Australia	33
Kangaroo Island	35
Western River Cove	37
Arkaroola	38
On the Way to the West	43
In the South-west of Western Australia	45
Other Parts of the World	49
Fiji	51
Arizona	52
East Anglia: Dunwich	54
Haiku Diary of a Trip to New Zealand	55
In Auckland	57
The Old and New Cathedrals	58
With the Quakers	59
Waitakere Forest Walk	60
Going North	61
North Again	63
South Again	65
South From Auckland	67
Wellington	79
To the South Island	81
Golden Bay	84
Still Going South	88
Christchurch	89

What is a haiku?

An aha! moment
caught in a few small words,
    a poetic hiccup

At Home in the Adelaide Hills

The Seasons

Spring

The river pool
is a mile deep…in it
    the clouds go down to heaven.

Outside the window
upside down
    a green insect doing push-ups.

A clump of iris
enjoying a late shower
    blossoms with snails.

The restless wind
sweeps winter's leaf litter
    under the carpet of spring.

Insects have laid bare
the architecture of a leaf,
    a lacy framework.

An ancient gum tree
hugs itself with branching arms
    to keep out the cold.

In the shadows
the creek flows red
    over a bed of willow roots.

A swamp hen's long-legged stride
awkwardly spans
    the stepping stones.

Two ducks together
waddling the rainy road…
    synchronised puttering.

Lilac trembles
as two honeyeaters
    explore its blossom.

In a waterfall of jasmine
a honeyeater
    hangs suspended.

The wattle bird sips
while upside down,
    looking unlikely.

Flattened in the grass
the cat looks up, guilty,
    from a fan of feathers.

In the grass
half a bird's egg,
    empty…

No one wants to hold
the smelly disconsolate
    rain-bedraggled cat.

A cloud of insects
drifts into a shaft of light
    and turns to gold.

Silver-eye hovers
in a blur of wing beats
    balancing the wind.

Before my eyes
a caterpillar drifts past,
    hanging by a thread.

After rain…
ankle-deep in a pool
    that holds half of the sky.

Long legs dangling
a heron gangles its way
    upwards into grace.

Walking on shadows
my feet move in and out
    of flickering branches.

Three geese
standing on three legs,
    silent heads bowed.

Trees blur
as cyclists zoom past…
    meanwhile, spring waits to be seen.

A small green shoot
having taken a wrong turn
    pushes through the floor.

Summer

Summer garden…
in the heat the clicks and pops
    of opening seed pods.

Far from home
and rose petals crisp
    in the summer heat.

In spiky spirals
this well-designed pine cone
    leads to the centre.

Fragrance of peaches
fills the whole kitchen
    and clings to my hands.

Wild mushrooms
lie heat exhausted on the bench
    gently oozing tar.

Ripening blackberries
by a dusty road…
    the scent of childhood.

Do not disturb…
a cobweb suspended
    from the clothes line.

Chainsaw season…
the valley vibrates
    to its strident whine.

A lopped-off tree stump
not knowing it was meant to die
    sprouts with new life.

Somewhere a bronze-wing
calls up haunted memories
    of another time.

Dampened earth drying…
breathing in eucalyptus…
    summer after rain.

A half-grown spinebill
up to the eyes in flower,
    looking for nectar.

In the dry creek bed
pebbles rattle
    having forgotten water.

At the road's edge
gum leaves lie stiff and black
    mummified in tar.

The old gum tree
clutches the bank
    with a fistful of gnarly roots.

Autumn

Autumn is here,
its glowing colours
    flaring through the rain.

White feathers fantailed,
puffed-out chest…
    dove on a letter box.

A weeping willow
mourns the passing of autumn
    with strings of golden tears.

Wood smoke and music
drifting and diffusing
    in still autumn air…

Out of the stillness
a wind begins to follow
    through the poplar tops.

Like festive lanterns
the poplar's translucent leaves
    are lit by the sun.

With a plop
a small floating log
    resolves into a platypus.

Crumbs of dirt still cling
to the brown toadstool
    that heaved through the earth last night.

On a sun-warmed car
a perching tabby finds
    a remnant of summer.

A wrinkle of smoke
drifts through still autumn air,
    making noses twitch.

Yesterday's bonfire…
smoke trickles
    down the bank.

Day's end…
the sky greys down,
air thins and stills.

Tiny spider web
held up for us to see
    by fingers of bamboo.

A strand of web
lifts with the breathing air
    and sunlight slides its length.

Leaves flutter and fall…
even the autumn sun
    has drifted down the sky.

Three geese
on three legs,
    silent heads bowed.

An inch of ripple,
foot after foot after foot…
    the caterpillar.

Approaching fast,
a busy upright tail
    wagging its dog.

Restless autumn sky…
a rainbow
    coming and going in the clouds.

Skeleton shadow
lies on the grass
    tied to a living tree.

Moving on…
boxes of yesterday
    wait with the garbage.

A passing insect
twitches a wrinkle
    on the glassy pond.

Bubbles cluster
by the waterfall,
    taking turns to pop.

On a dam
dusted with pollen
    a duck calligraphs its way.

Winter

Frost fronds underfoot
and mist steaming off the creek
    into chilly air…

Against the grey sky
plum blossom
    gleaming in the sun.

Among the violets
a sleeping cat is stirred
    by winter-fingered winds.

In the pre-dawn dark
a plover's melancholy cry
    calls me awake.

Grasses crisped with frost
outside a lighted window
    shine white in the dawn.

Winter's tears
blurring the trees outside…
    my window streaked with rain.

Black cockatoos
hold a creaking consultation
    high in a pine tree.

Clouds roll back
and sunlights trickles
    down the watery road.

Nine crested geese
paddling
    in Bogaduck Road.

Rain squalls air-brush
pine needle calligraphy
    on the wooden bridge.

Muddy lane…
in a footprint
    leaves float among the clouds.

A flash of blue
and twittering on the track ahead…
    a bounce of wrens.

After the rain,
two ducks floating
    on somebody's lawn.

On a leafless branch
twenty sparrows twittering
    in the winter sun.

Willow twigs
flex and dip
    under the weight of a rosella.

Fingers of sun
reach through the window
    and touch the sleeping cat.

Wings flickering,
honeyeater flirts
    with a grevillea.

Whiskered with lichens
twiggy branches hold
    the world in a raindrop.

Observed in Passing

Unseasonal Haiku

The pipe organ's roar
blasts us into space,
    by-passing the cathedral.

T'ai chi devotees
glide around the polished floor,
    avoiding pianos.

Whirling dervishes,
blown off course by gully winds,
    may have now reached heaven…

Newspaper faces…
children pressed against the mesh
    longing for parents.

The Discussion Group: haiku in response to issues

Capital punishment:
I live, he has to die.
    Who is the loser?

Euthanasia

Suffering
may bring enlightenment,
    but so may not suffering…

Cloning

I found the answer
    while talking to myself.

Do animals have souls?

The cat's soul and mine
speak to each other
    each time our eyes meet.

Do we need religious structures for spiritual development?

The bonsai lives
by the gardener's rule,
    beautiful but stunted.

Spiritual immaturity

Looking at the stars
through a telescope
    I see only my eyelash.

Future of the Earth and humanity

Glaciers melt,
mountains crumble to dust…
    We came. We go.

Fruit and Veg Haiku

Written to accompany paintings by Glen Ash

Eggs

Collecting the eggs…
the smooth round brown dome
    of the old farmer's head.

His bald head gleaming
the sage confers with his hens
    and gathers their eggs.

Lazy clouds float
in a summer sky…on the bench
    a blue bowl of eggs.

Chillies

A Chinese doorway
framed by strings of fire crackers…
    or are they chillies?

Gleaming red and green,
warning light or invitation?
    …aha! gotcha!

'Sample me!' they say,
invitation to the crunch…
    once bitten, twice shy.

Quinces

Solid in the hand
the quince entices the nose
    with its golden scent

Quinces and Apples

From flower to fruit…
in this bowl are memories
    of the orchard's year.

Red Onions

Self-importance fills
the bulging purple waistcoat
    of the red onion.

Tomatoes

So smooth of skin,
so red, so plump, so tasty…
    essence of summer.

Reds rule: democracy
is overtaken by
    tomato's sauce.

Pears

See in its smooth curves
the subtlety of the pear,
    style and taste its own.

Kohlrabi

The kohlrabi…who?
religious leader of the
    turnip-cabbage clan.

Figs

Was this succulent fruit
the one that tempted Eve?
    The leaf was handy too…

Velvet to the touch
this inside-out fruit
    is just a bunch of blossom.

On the Road in Australia

Kangaroo Island

Ghosts

Out there
    the waves are crashing on the rocks,
but here the only sound's
    the little crunch of shell-grit...

In the air
    a small cool breeze lifts
stirred-up smells of iodine and salt
    and ghosts of dead sea creatures...

On the sand
    the drift and sift of whitened shells,
the spiky black graffiti of dry seaweed,
    the orange loom of lichen-crusted rocks...

The pools,
    each one a window, still as glass,
with pebbles smooth as soap...
    In one a stranded crab,
big as my hand and not long dead,
    sprawls awkwardly across a rock,
its armour plating rich with purple-red and ochre.

Inch by wince
    my toes explore a limestone ridge
that jags out into the bay,
    a honeycomb of fossil bubbles.
Wedged into its tiny caves
    are bleaching shells
and lacy scraps of coral.

Upside down
    and jammed into a crack
a driftwood plank becomes
    a cemetery for barnacles,
the tiny headstones whitening with age
    and draped with strands
of toffee-coloured kelp
    that drip with tears of salt.

Western River Cove

Our tent stands on a small plateau,
and looks across the sleeping flank
    of summer's lazy grass-furred hills,
and downwards to
    an iced-tea creek that winds
around the corner to a tiny beach.

The hills rise up behind us,
    steep and round,
and in the afternoon the wind begins to blow.
It funnels down the valley,
looping over roller coaster hills
    and fills the tent.

The guy ropes creak and strain,
    the canvas flaps and bellies out.
Shortly we could be sailing back
    across Investigator Strait.
We might be home for tea.

Arkaroola

Yunta to Koonamore

A dried-up land
    whose stony bones
poke through a sunburned skin
    stubbled with silvery prickles…

Autumn and afternoon
have leached the colour from the day
    and flat against its washed-out backdrop
distant ranges stack themselves against the sky,
indigo to purple, blue to pale.

Sleeping Out

Black velvet sky
    and the stars so fresh and tingly
        you could inhale them
and sneeze out another Milky Way.

Cocooned in blankets and silence
    we watch the moon glide the sky
and tell the temperature by the tip of the nose

Arkaroola Campsite, Late Summer

A sandy riverbank by the ghost of a creek,
    and river gums,
cream and silver, golden-bronze and salmon-pink.

In the creek boulders are heaped,
and rocks, which we'd call pebbles in another place, but here
they might be porphyry, chalcedony or jasper.

By night we listen to the silence of the empty creek.
The full moon rises from behind a hill
    and chases Jupiter across the sky.

In the morning ravens wake us,
telling us the news.
It's all bad and they disapprove of everything.
Later, with a chorus of crickets
    and a corps de ballet of bush flies
the galahs arrive, to rosy up the world.

Echidna

Scuttle scuffle
    claws clicking
        snout sniffling
           someone's coming!
                startle hurtle
                  …*freeze*

                Dead stop
              shrink size
              hide snout
                hold breath
                    …*wait*

                    All clear
                      snout out
                        legs engage
                            trundle bundle
                                up the gully
                              …*go!*

Bararrana Gorge, Late Summer

At the bottom of the gorge, crusader-like,
I'm lying on a slab of rock
    and looking at the sky.
Here in the shade it's deep and cool,
    but high above me, on the rusty rim,
        a tiny grass-tree glints against a cobalt sky
        and in a lazy sweep an eagle rides the thermals.

The western wall
    catches the sun on tilting slabs of ochre red,
        precariously stacked…
a library of ancient books
    that tell the history of the gorge.

Memories of water…
a hundred million years of floods
    tossing enormous rocks like leaves,
settling slabs askew against the walls,
    drilling, gouging, sanding dips and hollows,
polishing smooth a monolith
    till now it feels like watered silk
delicate in pink and grey.

And here's a memory of the morning of the world:
    an ocean's ripple marks
        immortalised in stone.

The gorge's floor is choked and chinked with rocks,
    big enough to climb and small enough to sift,
        a treasure trove.
Pinks, from pale to rose, shot through with veins of quartz;
    a soft teal blue; the verdigris of copper;
        silver sparks of mica everywhere.

Last year it rained,
    a flooding rush,
but now the water's gone
and all that's left's a pool or two,
    still as the stones, a vivid yellow green;
and glued into the mud,
    a dozen yabby shells.

On the Way to the West

Whale Watching, Nullarbor Plain

It's spring, but here where ocean meets the cliffs
it's forty-one degrees.
A hot north-easter swirls the dust
and in the distance
lifts a sunlit haze of white above the sand dunes.

All around us, stretching flat,
a knee-high fuzz of prickly grey…

With a shove
the wind propels us down the path
and pushes fiercely at others coming back,
discomfited and pink from too much sun,
clutching haphazardly at cameras and hats.

At the platform jutting from the cliff,
    hanging over the sea,
we hold the rail,
brush off the circling flies
    and gaze.

Down there it's cool
shifting blues and crinkled lace of white,
and drifting in and out with lazy grace
a dozen whales.
From time to time they heave into our world of air.
The water foams from dark grey backs
then closes over as they sink or roll.
I think of elephants,
the massive dignity, the sheer impressiveness of size.
    The young, like children everywhere,
circle their idling mums and try their skills,
flipping a tail in casual showmanship.

And then the wind begins to change.
It swings south-west
and almost in a breath we sigh and straighten and relax.
The whales have noticed too,
become more purposeful.
They surge and roll…
and on the lazy surface of the sea
the crisp white waves begin.

In the South-west of Western Australia

Campground at Night, Lucky Bay

By eight o'clock it's dark
and everyone has gone into their tents
like snails into their shells
and battened down
and gone to bed.

It's then the sea takes over
and its all-pervading rumble fills the air
and thunders round the bay.
The wind, in sympathy,
shakes the tent walls,
vibrates the ropes and billows out the roof.
A lullaby for sleep.

Early Morning

We stride the early-morning beach,
still gleaming from the tide that washed out yesterday.
Now on the fine white sand
there's just a strand of weed
and two neat bird-feet prints.
That's all.

Wet Walk, Porrongorups

Gleaming in the mist
the karri trees reach straight and smooth into the clouds,
ivory columns lifting
from cocoons of rough grey bark.

By the path
attention-getting swags of hovea,
blue-purple in the fresh green wetness of new leaves,
and on the track a flash of scarlet
as rosellas settle, scatter and reform
then disappear in a kaleidoscopic moment.

Up…
the laboured breath of climbing
pulling in damp air and eucalyptus…
Overhead, the plaintive creaks of cockatoos.

The mist comes down as we ascend
until we stand at last high on a rocky dome
    enfolded by a cloud,
our world contained by pearly light.
The rock face trickles damp,
cushioned with moss and glowing pink and white
    with sheets of tiny flowers.

The rain is harder now,
filling pockets in the rock,
trickling into channels
     and cascading down the track.
Our path becomes a tunnel through the scrub
where hakea and head-high thryptomene
     laden with flowers and rain
shower-bath us as we pass.

Crouching for shelter in a twiggy cave
we watch the water funnel off a branch
and in the moss, behind a stone,
find tiny hidden orchids.

Climbing down
we meet a mob of children coming up,
as wet as fish and loving it,
     (or some of them),
while at the rear the stragglers damply sag.
'Isn't this great!'
their teachers say, through clinging strands of hair.
'I said to wear wet weather gear!' says one of them,
himself well-dressed in bathers, anorak and boots.

The track has turned into a stony creek.
We slither down a rock that waterfalls with rain
and find our feet on dirt and bark again…
and suddenly, we're back.

Other Parts of the World

Fiji

The Sleeping Giant

(a mountain range near Nadi)

His bones are rock,
his fingers bound by vines,
his craggy toes poke through the clouds,
and centuries ago his ears were stopped by falling stones.
Storm rains trickling down his nose
    do not disturb.

The Garden of the Sleeping Giant

A hundred shades of green
in spiky whorls and flaring fans,
in leafy plumes that arch and arabesque their way over the path;
or tiny flattened circles,
    damp against the moss,
or spears that point the way
to massive trunks spreading their limbs against the sky,
half-hidden in translucent clouds of leaves;
and vines that convolute their way up any likely tree,
clutching the bark with predatory arms
before they cascade down again,
streamers of heart-shaped leaves that stir in any breeze.

Arizona

Grand Canyon in the Mist

Just by our feet
a juniper has taken root
and twists, with casual bonsai grace,
over the canyon rim.

Today it hangs in mist,
and everywhere we look
our eyes see silence.

Canyon De Chelly... The Anasazi and Us

The land behind us flattens out
in shades of palest rose,
lifting to mesas, springtime blue,
their tops ruled straight and clean against the sky.

Here at our feet the land has split apart
and red cliffs tumble for a thousand feet,
down to a haze of green beside the watercourse
    that skeins its way across the valley floor.
Opposite, the cliffs rise up again
    from tumbled fans of scree.
The canyon walls are pocked with caves,
    creviced with cracks,
a thousand hiding places for a people long since gone.

Who was their enemy, those Ancient Ones?
Why did they build their mud-wasp nests,
    their cell-like homes,
in slots a hundred feet or five
    above the canyon floor?
What did they fear?

In the end
    the enemy they planned against
was not the one that drove them out,
no rush of fierce and stealthy raiders in the night,
but long, slow siege by famine and by drought.

East Anglia: Dunwich

An ordinary pebble beach
banks itself in lazy curves
    down to a glassy sea.
Spreadeagled on the stones and basking with intent
a sunbather, uncomfortably pink,
protects his dignity by blanking out the rest of us.
Behind us,
    crumbling quietly to itself,
a sandy cliff dissolves into the sea.

Six hundred years ago a town was here.
Its streets and markets clustered round the bay,
stretching its quays
like fingers of a hand
        into the sea.
Then tides swept in and storm-waves ate the land.
The town was swallowed at a single gulp.

A hundred years ago
a church fell slowly off the cliff,
    leaving the tower
        which they moved inland.

There's still a village here
behind the dunes.
It looks secure and cosy
    in the English way…
As safe as houses.

Haiku Diary of a Trip to New Zealand

In this diary I used the haiku form as a shorthand way to tell the story of what we saw and did.

In Auckland

Spring in Auckland…
streets awash with rain
    and blossom.

Magnolias,
each bloom so perfect
    we stop to wonder.

Acrobatic artistry…
tuis soar and dive
    as we trudge below.

'No mountain bikes please'…
On this retired volcano
    only tourists throng.

The Old and New Cathedrals

The old wooden church
rolled its way across the street
    then settled its joints.

Under the lectern
questing fingers find
    a wooden mouse is hiding.

The old church
is cave-like but gleaming …
    reverence contained.

The new church…
a celebration in stained glass
    and light-bringing space.

With the Quakers

End of a long day…
we return at dusk
    welcomed in by Quaker warmth.

Into the silence
of the meeting
    a baby sings its ministry.

Waitakere Forest Walk

The plant book now
has soggy leaves…souvenir
    of a rainy walk.

Listening for birds…
not a chirp to hear until
    the deluge passes.

Going North

Auckland to Russell

Public works query:
'How many roadworks can be
    fitted into spring?'

Russell, Bay of Islands

Once a hellhole,
now a tourist haven…
    Darwin would be surprised.

Morepork at night,
tui for the morning call,
    pukekos at dusk…

Waitangi

Crossing the bay,
morning sun and frisking breeze
    on an open deck.

Walking to Waitangi…
it seems like the right way
    to approach history.

On Reconciliation, 1838-style

The King must have thought
that one good British man
    was equal to the job.

Christ Church at Russell

Gravestones in the grass...
Maori and Pakeha,
    blood spilt together...

In this family,
pioneers in their new land,
    six children died.

The Printery (Pompalier House, Russell), 1840

The men of God gave life and work
to print the word of God
    for men.

In the tanning vats
skins became leather...
    in the walls, mummified rats.

North Again

Whangaroa

A bay full of boats…
We didn't climb to St Paul's
    but laughed at seagulls.

To Cape Reinga

Sand as white and fine
as icing sugar
    and a handful of new shells…

We meet 'summer cows':
some are brown, some are black,
    some are just cows.

In a land once full
of Dalmatian gum-diggers,
    avocados rule.

White-plumed invaders
march their way over the hill…
    the Pampas army.

At this rocky cape
oceans meet and spirits leave
    to find their way home.

Tapotupotu Bay

Not only seagulls
but chaffinches and small quails
    come to our picnic.

Small balls of feathers
bob and weave at ankle-height
    with one intent…crumbs.

Ninety-mile Beach

Sand-boarding the dunes…
getting high slowly
    to get low quickly.

Firm sand, mist and spray…
the bus hisses at high speed
    along the beach.

Baby seal stranded…
we turn back, take photographs,
    exclaim, and forget.

Hoof prints on the sand…
all that's left of wild horses
    as the mist comes down.

South Again

Waipapakauri via Dargaville to Auckland

The long day starts
with common sense advice
    from a muesli packet.

At Arihapu
we find we didn't need
    to come here after all.

Winding our way
through kilometres of
    wrinkled green paddocks…

Little houses perch on hills,
not quite sliding off…
    One day they might.

Any moment now,
    around another corner,
        we'll see Footrot Flats…

        but no – it's Koho Koho,
            a neat little town with a ferry
            and a

sophisticated
art gallery to catch the
passing tourist trade.

The general store
has good Anzac biscuits and,
    of course, fish hooks.

A long sunny glide
across a wide still inlet…
    …a distant white spire.

The Giant Kauri…
its presence even bigger
    than its size.

South From Auckland

Hamilton Botanic Gardens

The Japanese Garden

> Each piece of gravel,
> each rock, is precision-placed,
> every tree sculpted.

The Chinese Garden

> Reflections…
> shadows of the real
> or something more?

The Indian Garden

> Contained and bordered…
> a living carpet of flowers
> in a marble frame.

The Renaissance Garden

> It's plain to see
> that symmetry delights the eye
> in plan and plantings.

The English Arts and Crafts Garden

> A lot of hard work
> to create a natural
>   and artless look…

The Kitchen Garden

> How satisfying
> how robust its plants,
>   row by row by row…

The Kiwi House, Otorohanga

>Businesslike, the kiwi
>trots and snuffles through the mulch
>in its pretend night.

Waitomo Caves

In our small party
>just us and a French student
>and a chatty guide.

>>*Topics we covered:*
>>*agriculture, history,*
>>*linguistics, caves...*

>>>*...genealogy*
>>>*and Scottish ancestry and*
>>>*Breton village life...*

>>>>*...the origin of Man,*
>>>>*Pacific migration trends*
>>>>*and, of course, glow worms.*

In between talking
we bump up a gravel road
      and look at the view…

…a hilly landscape,
green and full of ups and downs
      and rocky outcrops…

Goats and turkeys
interspersed with sheep…
      a feral hillside.

Down the hill…
tall trees hung with lichen
      rise to meet us.

Damp moss underfoot…
wet ferns and a rushing creek…
      childhood memories…

In the caves

Darkness and silence…
the gentle slosh of water
    moving past the boat…

Our eyes read the dark…
overhead a million stars
    sprinkle the cave roof.

A break from wonder…
outside, with hot chocolate,
    we sit and talk.

Cave Two: we walk it…
no stars here, just stalactites
    which loom and drip.

Sometimes, looking up,
an air shaft high above,
    a pile of bones below…

Waitomo to Rotorua

As we travel south
a rolling wave of magnolias
    comes with us.

A smug countryside…
green pastures, prosperity,
    self-satisfaction…

A corrugated iron
dog and sheep and shepherd?
    Too right, it's sculpture.

Rotorua

Steaming thermal pools
neatly contained
    in an Edwardian park…

Juggling umbrellas and cameras
to capture the steam
    in the rain…

Aha! We find that
deep under the volcanoes
    lurks a Balrog!

People soon deduced
that if it smelt so awful
    it should do them good…

Waiotapu

Waters hiss, mud boils…
crude oil and graphite
    arsenic and mercury…

Sulphur everywhere,
yellow streaks and crystals on rocks
    and in the air…

All shades of green,
delicate to dirty and
    verdant to verdigris…

The word might have
been invented just to describe
    boiling mud-pools…
        'Plop!'

Feeding the geyser,
the guide times his speech and moves
    just before she blows.

In nomenclature
it seems the Devil's got a lot
    to answer for.

The Buried Village

Remains of a town,
tragic once, now idyllic…
    all the ghosts have gone.

All that's left,
some mud-encrusted plates,
    a fireplace or two…

Rotorua to Wanganui

Through mist and rain
a looming glimpse of
    snow-streaked mountains.

Hovering over the telegraph poles
a low-level fuzz
    of rainbow.

From the Desert Road
a speckled fur of tussocks
    covers the low hills.

'Army land. Keep out!'
Sooner or later
    an explosion will occur.

Mt Ruapehu

It rains and it rains.
We stop. It stops.
    Up the mountain, quick!

Rimu, ferns and beech
shrink as we climb higher,
    from giants to dwarves…

Before the road's end
the clouds come down to meet us…
    trailed by mist, we walk.

Twisty trees drip mist
and lichen…we find the falls
    by the sound of the roar.

The Long Road to Wanganui

The roads winds down
through a tumble of steep-sided hills
    to meet the sea.

Cattle and sheep graze
at improbabl angles…
    they must be glued there.

Wattle jubilates,
quietly pleased at its
    successful invasion…

Foxton

A windmill…
its shadow flickers while the blades
    swish overhead.

Our souvenirs…
good advice, wholemeal flour
    and a dusty handprint.

Kapiti Coast

At a hidden house
enfolded by its garden
    we find a welcome.

A flourish of ferns
admires its own reflection
    in a tranquil pool.

The Back Road to Wellington

Steep, narrow, winding…
a forested tunnel
    that leads to Rivendell.

At a pause for breath
we find we're parking next to
    a panache of peacocks…

The regal brilliance!
his rear, though also handsome,
    could be another bird.

Wellington

'Lots of scenery
and very close together'...
    a local comment.

The streets convolute,
the hills are steep, the houses cling
    against the odds.

We drive the coast road
where wind, rain and waves
    compete with us for leeway.

Weatherboard houses,
stilted and balconied
    and nailed to the hillside...

In the old Bond Store
a pretend cat's tail twitches
    at a pretend rat.

Earthquake instructions
at the Quaker guest house...
    how appropriate.

The Botanic Gardens

Rising quietly
through a tunnel of leaves and mist…
    the cable car.

Beautiful gardens, icy breeze…
hot chocolate
    saves us again.

To the South Island

In the ferry line
wind gusts rattle campervans...
    even seagulls hop.

Breaking up the Sound
criss-crossed by Cook
    a jigsaw of islands...

As we glide by islands,
old whaling bays, steep hills,
    some watch the movie...

Nelson

In the grim grey church
fort-like on its hill
    a bunch of ladies t'ai chi...

Looking friendlier
the Quaker meeting house
    sits lower down the slope.

Cuckoo-clock cottage
and look who just popped out...
    the sun-seeking owner.

In his pieces
the glass-blower
    caught all the colours of the world.

The jolly potter
sings as he works and has
    a shop stocked with his wares…

Over the Tech. door –
are they eagles or vultures?
    I'd go in the back…

Across the dawn sky
an invisible jet
    tugs its vapour trail.

Nelson to Pohara by Way of Takaka Hill

We corkscrew our way
up a hill, stopping
    on top to wonder.

Shards of marble scales
from a mythical monster
    litter the hilltop…

Geology combines
with mythology
    to make a good story.

Plunging down the hill
we arrive at the bottom:
    Upper Takaka.

Golden Bay

Pohara Beach

Sunset on damp sand…
shells cast long shadows
    and dogs chase their own.

To say I was here
I collect a scallop shell…
    an old pilgrim trick.

Wainui Falls

Eyes on the track ahead…
roots, earth, fallen leaves…
    overhead, the ferns.

The fall's roar is loud…
its breath makes us shiver,
    its mist makes a rainbow.

The Grove

Dwarfing us
roots as big as tree trunks
    flow round giant rocks.

The lookout…
sheep graze, white dots on a billiard table…
    a small dead lamb.

The Old Cemetery

Old graves
under old trees
    undisturbed a hundred years…

Early gravestones say
the pioneers 'went to sleep'…
    later, they just died.

Farewell Spit

Coffee, scones and birds
at the Paddle Crab Café…
    sun on Farewell Spit.

Walk to Fossil Point

Young lambs are whiter,
friskier and springier
    than their staid mothers.

On the other side of the fence
lambs
    are always bleatier.

Standing on one leg
a pukeko stops to let
    sheep and lamb pass by.

Once house and garden
now just fireplace, giant trees
    and arum lilies.

Wide white ocean beach
with nobody there but us
    and a grumpy seal.

Not one fossil...
but ammonite descendants
    are almost as good!

Still Going South

Hamer Springs

From the steaming pool
we see snow-covered mountains
      and watch the stars come out.

Waiau Bridge Bungee jumpers

Watching the young leap,
at a respectful distance…
      with binoculars.

Turquoise river,
flying launch, white wave, sharp turn,
      near miss, screams of joy.

Christchurch

Botanic Gardens

The cherry blossom
attracts bumble bees as well as
    photographers.

Statue of a gent
oversees the gardens' gate…
    Watch your step in here!

The Time Ball Tower at Lyttleton

Castle on a hill,
time ball on the castle roof,
    all eyes on the ball…

Time To Go Home: Christchurch Airport

An award
for the most laid-back airport
    in this hemisphere…

www.ingramcontent.com/pod-product-compliance
Lightning Source LLC
Chambersburg PA
CBHW062141100526
44589CB00014B/1652